P9-DCC-916

5199

PERFECT PETS

Rabbits

Kathryn Hinds

BENCHMARK BOOKS

MARSHALL CAVENDISH

NEW YORK

Benchmark Books
Marshall Cavendish Corporation
99 White Plains Road
Tarrytown, New York 10591

Library of Congress Cataloging-in-Publication Data
Hinds, Kathryn, date
Rabbits / by Kathryn Hinds.
p.   cm. — (Perfect Pets)
Includes bibliographical references (p.   ).
Summary: Describes the habits, characteristics, and history of rabbits, their use in folklore, and their raising as a pet.
ISBN 0-7614-0793-6
1. Rabbits—Juvenile literature. [1. Rabbits.] I. Title. II. Series.
SF453.2.H55   1999   636.9'322—DC21   97-40462   CIP   AC

Photo research by Ellen and Matthew Dudley

Cover photo: *Photo Researchers, Inc.:* Tim Davis
Back cover photo: *Norvia Behling*

The photographs in this book are used by permission and through the courtesy of: *Animals Animals:* Reneé Stockdale, 4; Niall Benvie, 5, 30; Stouffer Productions, 21; S. Michael Bisceglie 12 (top); Geo. F. Godfary, 14; Reed/Williams, 17; Gerard Lacz, 18 (top); Oxford Scientific Films, 18 (bottom); Robert Maier, 19, 28; *Norvia Behling:* title page, 7, 10, 12 (bottom), 13, 15, 16, 20, 22, 24, 25, 27, 29; *Photofest:* Warner Bros, Inc., 8; *Photo Researchers, Inc.:* Jeanne White, 3; George Haling, 26; *F. Warne & Co. 1902, 1987:* 9.

Printed in Hong Kong
6   5   4   3   2   1

To Jane Hinds,
my mother-in-law and fellow Beatrix Potter fan,

and Dudley Hinds,
my father-in-law and fellow writer

The rabbit on the left has stood up on its hind legs to get a better look around, while its sibling is in a resting position.

With

their long ears, wiggly noses, and powder-puff tails, rabbits make some of the cutest pets around. But there's a lot more to rabbits than cuteness. In myths and folklore from all over the world, rabbits and their close relatives, hares, are creatures of magic, power, and cunning.

From ancient times people in many places have looked at the full moon and seen the shape of a rabbit on its surface. In Chinese myths it is said that the rabbit who lives on the moon makes a potion that gives eternal life. Japanese stories tell how the rabbit on the moon pounds rice to make rice cakes, which are sometimes described as children. A Korean poem portrays the moon as a ship sailed by a white rabbit, and from India there is an old saying, "The moon leaps like a hare when the sun dies."

A wild European rabbit

The Aztec people of Mexico also saw a rabbit in the moon, and the lakes around which they built Mexico City had the same rabbit shape. Because of this the Aztecs sometimes described the earth as "face-up rabbit." In Central America the Mayan people worshiped Ixchel (eesh-CHEL), goddess of the moon, childbirth, and weaving. Her special companion was a rabbit.

Rabbits are among the first animals to give birth in the spring, and they continue to have many babies throughout the summer. Because of this, in many parts of the world rabbits became symbols of springtime, rebirth, and abundant life.

Fifteen hundred years ago people in England honored a goddess of dawn and springtime called Eostre (ee-OH-streh). The word *Easter* comes from her name, because that holiday is celebrated at the same time of year as Eostre's ancient festival. The Easter bunny was originally Eostre's hare: Legend tells how the goddess once found a bird in the snow, its wings frozen. To save the bird, she turned it into a hare—a hare who still had a bird's ability to lay eggs! The eggs were brightly colored, and the goddess gave them to children as presents.

The Ojibway and Menominee Indians of North America have traditional stories about Manabozho (mah-nah-BOH-zhoh), "White Rabbit."

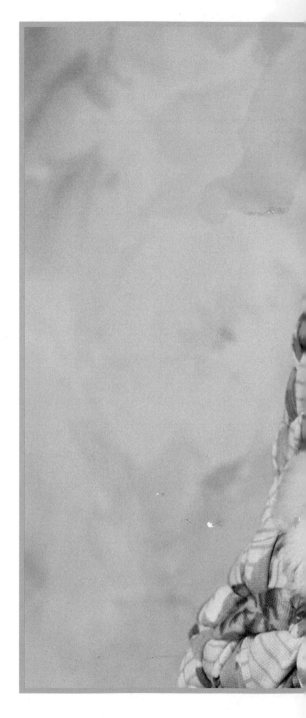

Baby rabbits, like these two Rex bunnies in an Easter basket, are an ancient symbol of spring.

Manabozho invented many things, from ball games to healing ceremonies. He was also a trickster. In fact, stories from many different Native American groups describe Rabbit as the cleverest and trickiest of animals. In much of Africa, too, Rabbit has been a popular trickster character in stories.

Bugs Bunny carries on a long tradition of stories about rabbits who use their cleverness to outwit enemies.

African-American slaves in the southeastern United States continued African storytelling traditions. The slaves developed the character of Brer Rabbit, whose cleverness constantly gets him in and out of trouble. Though he is small, Brer Rabbit is able to trick and outwit every other animal, even Mr. Man. But the most famous tricky rabbit today is probably Bugs Bunny, whose cartoon adventures entertain people of all ages. Rabbit stories have been part of human culture for thousands of years, and anyone lucky enough to spend time with rabbits will soon begin to understand why.

The Creator of Peter Rabbit

One of the most famous and beloved rabbit stories in the world is Beatrix Potter's *The Tale of Peter Rabbit,* published in 1902 with color illustrations by the author. Potter was born in England in 1866. She began drawing and painting plants and animals when she was a child. Her career as an artist began in 1890 with a Christmas card picture of her pet rabbit, Benjamin. Peter Rabbit, the star of her first book, was based on another of her rabbit friends, Peter Piper. She went on to write twenty-two more books for children, including *The Tale of Benjamin Bunny, The Tale of the Flopsy Bunnies,* and *The Story of a Fierce Bad Rabbit.*

Peter Rabbit helps himself to some radishes—and gets into big trouble—in Mr. McGregor's garden.

No matter how pampered a pet rabbit may be, it will still have the wild heart of its ancestors.

Rabbits

of one sort or another live in most parts of the world, in every type of **habitat**, from desert to marsh to arctic tundra. The most common wild rabbit in North America is the cottontail. All **domestic** rabbits—the kind that become pets—are descended from European wild rabbits. They originally came from lands around the western Mediterranean Sea.

The ancient Romans raised wild rabbits for food, keeping them in outdoor pens. Roman soldiers and colonists took rabbits with them to many parts of Europe. Rabbits were finally tamed by French monks during the Middle Ages. In the sixteenth century people began to develop different **breeds**, or types, of domestic rabbits. Today there are close to fifty rabbit breeds.

Pet rabbits are found in a great variety of sizes and colors. The largest breed is the Flemish giant—it is bigger than most cats. The Netherland dwarf is the smallest of all rabbits. It has very short ears and comes in twenty-one different colors and color combinations. Dwarf rabbits are often highly energetic.

One of the most popular types of pet rabbit is the Dutch. This small breed is always white around the middle of its body, but there is a contrasting color on the back half of the body and spreading from the cheeks to the tips of the ears. Another favorite pet is the New Zealand, which is medium sized and may be white, red, or black.

Most domestic rabbits have fur that is about an inch long, but the fur of rex and satin rabbits is roughly half that.

A Flemish giant at rest.

This ruby-eyed white Netherland dwarf is ready to leap away at a moment's notice.

The Year of the Rabbit

In China there is an ancient tradition of astrology, the study of how the positions of the stars and planets affect human lives. In this tradition each year is ruled by one of twelve different animals. One of these animals is the rabbit. Anyone born in 1975, 1987, 1999, and so on is considered to have been born in the Year of the Rabbit. (Keep in mind that the Chinese year begins in January or February.) These "Rabbits" are said to be lucky, kind, intelligent, artistic, generous, and comfort loving. They may sometimes be self-centered, moody, or distrustful, but are usually peaceful.

A Holland lop. This type of lop-eared rabbit is not much bigger than the Netherland dwarf.

The fur of rex rabbits resembles plush or thick velvet, while satin rabbits' fur has a unique sheen. Both breeds appear in a variety of colors, including some unusual ones, such as lilac (a purplish gray) for the rex and copper for the satin.

The longest rabbit fur of all belongs to angoras. This

silky fur must be clipped every three months and can be spun into a soft, luxurious yarn. Angora rabbits make excellent pets, too, as they are usually very gentle and affectionate. They are small to medium in size.

Lops are the most unusual-looking domestic rabbits. Their long, floppy ears do not stand up straight but droop down. Lops often have rather stubborn personalities, but they can also be very lively.

Many pet rabbits are **mongrels** that do not belong to any particular breed. But mongrel or purebred, every domestic rabbit has something special to offer to a loving family.

Above: *A French angora. Its wool is often blended with sheep's or goat's wool (mohair) to make extremely soft sweaters.*

Opposite: *Lops come in many colors and color combinations.*

A baby rabbit stops to smell the flowers. Caring for a pet rabbit gives a person the chance to enjoy life's simple pleasures, too.

One

thing that makes a rabbit such an interesting and special pet is the fact that domestic rabbits behave just like wild ones. Watching and learning to understand a pet rabbit brings a person closer to nature. Caring for a rabbit also reminds us of the importance of kindness, gentleness, patience, and taking time to appreciate the little things in life.

Wild rabbits are hunted by a number of **predators**, so they have evolved many traits to help them survive. Domestic rabbits have inherited most of these traits. Rabbits are extremely alert—they can even sleep with their eyes open. They can see almost all the way around themselves without turning their heads. Their long ears can move to pick up the smallest sounds from any direction. Their constantly wiggling noses detect and identify the scents of both enemies and friends.

The rabbit's keen sense of smell is one of its best defenses against danger.

Rabbits are always watching, listening, and sniffing. When a rabbit senses danger, it may freeze, hoping to blend in with its surroundings. More often, though, it will run, leaping in a wild zigzag pattern that is designed to confuse a predator. Both wild and domestic rabbits also seem to enjoy running, hopping, and leaping for their own sakes. It can be very entertaining to watch a pet rabbit bound around the house or yard!

European wild rabbits dig underground rooms and tunnels, called **warrens**, where they can be safe from danger and raise their young. A group of eight to fifteen rabbits lives together in a warren. One male and one female are **dominant**—they are like the king and queen. Only the queen may raise her babies inside the warren; other females have to go somewhere else to dig their nests.

Domestic rabbits are also excellent diggers. They, too,

A European wild rabbit pauses at the entrance to its warren.

These baby dwarf rabbits are staying close to their mother for now, but in just a few months they will be adults themselves.

like to have safe, dark, enclosed places to go to. They are happiest if they can have at least one other rabbit for company. However, male rabbits will usually fight with each other, just as wild male rabbits fight to be dominant. Both wild and domestic rabbits can become quite feisty if they feel that their territory is being invaded. They can bite, kick, and scratch with amazing strength and fierceness for such small animals. But unless they feel threatened or are treated unkindly, pet rabbits are always peaceful and gentle.

Rabbits mark their territory by rubbing their chins on landmarks—twigs and stones outdoors, furniture and food

Is the carrot a snack or a toy? For this baby rabbit, it's both!

A snowshoe hare in its winter coat; in summertime its fur is brown. This hare is most common in Canada.

Rabbits or Hares?

Rabbits and hares belong to the same animal family. They look so much alike that it can be hard to tell them apart—plus some types of hares and rabbits have confusing names. The jack rabbit, for example, is a hare, while the Belgian hare is actually a breed of domestic rabbit! So what's the difference between hares and rabbits? Hares are born with fur and open eyes, but rabbits are born naked and blind. In addition, hares are usually larger than wild rabbits and have longer ears and legs.

bowls indoors. In the safety and familiarity of its territory, a rabbit will hop around in a relaxed way, now and then stopping to sniff or listen to something interesting. Rabbits love to explore their surroundings and will rise up on their hind legs to get a better look around.

Rabbits are generally very quiet animals. They communicate mainly through body language. A rabbit that is feeling completely at ease will lie on its stomach with its legs stretched out behind it. A very contented rabbit may even roll on the ground. When a rabbit nudges your hand with its nose, it is saying "Hello" or "Please pet me." Sometimes a rabbit will softly grind its teeth while you are petting it—this is its way of purring. But if it pushes your hand away or shakes its ears while being held or petted, it is saying "That's enough now." A rabbit who is squatting or lying in a relaxed way with its ears folded back is resting and does not want to be disturbed. When a rabbit stamps or drums its feet, something has frightened it.

Opposite: *An unusual friendship. Rabbits cannot always live safely with cats or dogs, who have strong hunting instincts.*

Baby lops crowd around a bowl of rabbit pellets, nutritionally complete food that contains dry vegetables, alfalfa, grains, and seeds.

Rabbits

make wonderful house pets because they are cute, clean, quiet, affectionate, and full of personality. But they do have some special needs. First, a pet rabbit must have a place that is its very own. Usually this will be a cage, and it should be *at least* four times as large as the full-grown animal. The cage ought to be placed in an area where the rabbit will not be disturbed by lots of noise or bothered by drafts. In one corner of the cage there should be a litter box full of hay or some other material that is safe to nibble on. This litter box needs to be cleaned once a day.

A water bottle, filled with fresh water every day, should be hung on the side of the cage. There should also be a rack

This English Spot has a safe and roomy enclosure on a porch.

25

full of alfalfa, timothy, or oat hay, which is very important for a rabbit's health. Hay is also excellent to chew on. Rabbits greatly enjoy chewing and need to do so in order to wear down their front teeth, which never stop growing. (In addition, rabbits can be given apple, willow, aspen, or pine branches to exercise their teeth on, as long as none of these woods have been treated with any kind of chemicals.) Besides hay, pet rabbits must be fed nutritionally balanced rabbit food. They can also have fresh fruits and vegetables (but

These baby wild rabbits at an animal rescue agency enjoy the same food as their domestic cousins.

no beans or rhubarb) in small amounts.

For a pet rabbit to be a truly happy and affectionate member of the family, it must be free to hop around outside its cage for at least half an hour a day. The rabbit must be closely watched during this time—and watching a pet rabbit is a great part of the fun of having one! The area where the rabbit is allowed to roam must be very safe. There should be no electrical cords or poisonous plants where it might chew them. With patience, most adult rabbits can be taught to use a litter box when they are outside the cage.

Naturally, pet rabbits also enjoy spending time outdoors whenever possible. But they should be kept absolutely safe from predators, including neighborhood dogs and cats. If a pet rabbit must live outside, it needs a secure pen that it cannot dig its way out of and that other animals cannot get into. The pen must be sheltered from wind and direct sunlight. Inside the pen there should be a hutch or little house where a rabbit can go for privacy and for shelter from bad weather.

This is the proper way to hold a rabbit—gently but securely, close to your body, and supporting the hindquarters. Never pick a rabbit up by the ears.

How to Choose a Pet Rabbit

This adorable baby Netherland dwarf will not grow very large, but it is likely to be rather high-strung. It would be happiest in a very calm household.

What should you look for if you want to get a rabbit? First, an adult is usually a better choice than a baby—that way you will be able to know the rabbit's full-grown size and mature personality from the start. Adult rabbits are also easier to train to use a litter box. Next, medium-size or large rabbits tend to be calmer and more manageable than dwarf types. Another thing you should consider is that rabbits are social animals. You may want to get two rabbits so that they can keep each other company—two sisters would probably get along best. No matter what, make sure a rabbit is healthy before you decide to make it your pet. It should have bright, clear eyes; its nose should not be runny; and its large top and bottom teeth should meet.

One of the most important things in caring for a pet rabbit is to take the time to learn to understand this unique animal. Rabbits are extremely sensitive. They respond to the way they are treated. If they are handled roughly they may get hurt, and they will probably not be very friendly. But a rabbit that is treated with gentleness and understanding will respond with real affection for its human companions. This unconditional love is one of life's most precious gifts.

*R*abbit Fun

Rabbits are very playful and energetic animals. They like to have things to crawl under, climb on, and hop around. They enjoy digging, chewing, and sometimes even picking things up in their teeth and throwing them. Some good rabbit toys are:

- A closed cardboard box with a couple of rabbit-size holes cut out of it.
- A box or natural willow basket full of shredded newspaper, straw, or dried leaves.
- Hard plastic baby keys.
- The hard plastic caps from laundry detergent bottles (well rinsed, of course).
- Cardboard tubes from toilet paper or paper towel rolls.
- Any toy (such as plastic balls) that can be rolled or tossed.

Toys and activities help keep a rabbit's mind and body in shape—and watching a rabbit play is fun for humans, too!

Fun Facts

🐰 Rabbits are most active in the morning and evening.

🐰 A male rabbit is called a buck, a female rabbit is called a doe, and baby rabbits are called bunnies.

🐰 A rabbit's pregnancy lasts for about thirty-one days.

🐰 Rabbits are fully adult at the age of four months.

🐰 A well-cared-for pet rabbit can live eight to twelve years.

🐰 A rabbit's tail is called a scut.

🐰 A domestic rabbit can hop faster than a white-tailed deer, a cat, or a person can run.

Glossary

breed: A group of animals that are descended from the same ancestors and share the same basic characteristics, including the way they look.

domestic: Describes the type of animal that has been tamed and trained to live among humans and help them.

dominant: Top ranking or in control.

habitat: The area or kind of environment in which an animal normally lives.

mongrel: An animal that doesn't belong to a particular breed; a mixed-breed animal.

predator: An animal that hunts other animals for food.

warren: A network of underground rooms and tunnels where wild European rabbits live.

Find Out More About Rabbits

ASPCA Pet Care Guides for Kids: Rabbit, by Mark Evans. New York: Dorling Kindersley, 1992.

Hamsters and Rabbits, by Dr. Michael Fox. New York: Tulchin Studios and Maier Communications, 1989. (videotape)

House Rabbit Handbook, 3rd edition, by Marinell Harriman. Alameda, California: Drollery Press, 1995.

Rabbits: A Complete Pet Owner's Manual, by Monika Wegler. Hauppauge, New York: Barron's, 1990.

Your First House Rabbit, by Marinell Harriman. Alameda, California: Drollery Press, 1994. (videotape)

Your Rabbit: A Kid's Guide to Raising and Showing. Pownal, Vermont: Storey Communications, 1992.

You may also wish to contact the House Rabbit Society, 1524 Benton Street, Alameda, CA 94501, or visit their web site: http://www.rabbit.org.

About the Author

Kathryn Hinds grew up near Rochester, New York, and always wanted to be a writer. She has been an animal lover ever since she was given her first pet, a kitten, when she was three years old. After college she lived in an apartment house that would not allow dogs or cats, so she had a pet rabbit. Ms. Hinds now lives on two acres in Georgia's Blue Ridge Mountains with her husband, their son, three cats, and two dogs. Her books for children include one about pet cats and several about the Romans, the Vikings, and other cultures of the past.